SIMPLE
RECIPES,
YOUR BEST
RESULTS

40+ Delicious Recipes
To Reach Your Goals

ISAGENIX®

Editorial Director and Content Creation: Mona Dolgov
Book Design: Leslie Anne Feagley
Copywriters: Karen Bedard and Laurie Asmus
Food Photography: Gary Sloan
Food Stylist: George Simons
Recipe Development: Mona Dolgov and Stephen Delaney

Library of Congress Cataloging-in-Publication Data has been applied for.
ISBN - 978-1-5323-7226-1

10   9   8   7   6   5   4   3   2   1

First Edition

Printed in Canada

*If you are pregnant, nursing, diabetic, on medication, have a medical condition, or are beginning
a weight-control program, consult your physician before using Isagenix products or making any other dietary changes.
Discontinue use if adverse events occur.

**Weight loss should not be considered typical. In a study performed in 2012 by University of Illinois at Chicago researchers,
subjects lost an average of 9 pounds with an average of 2 pounds of the loss from visceral fat after 30 days on an Isagenix System.
The subjects also had a greater level of adherence and had more consistent weight loss from week to week compared
to subjects on a traditional diet.

†These statements have not been evaluated by the Food and Drug Administration.
These products are not intended to diagnose, treat, cure, or prevent any disease.

The 50- and 100-calorie portions mentioned are +/-10% in calories.

YOUR BEST LIFE BEGINS IN 5...4...3...2...

One life. It's all we get. And we want to make it easier for you to get the most out of it. To step up to every challenge. To push into exciting new comfort zones. So we made this guide filled with recipes and tips to help you achieve your health goals. That includes tasty shake switch-ups, quick-prep snacks, and meals with 400- to 600-calories. Enjoy delicious one-pan meals in less than 30 minutes and sweet and savory snacks made with nutritious, easy-to-find ingredients. Grab life by the fork!

TABLE OF CONTENTS

SHAKES

HAVE YOUR SHAKE AND EAT IT, TOO.

These tasty new recipes and quick tips make getting your instant nutrition easier (and more fun) than ever. And get this—your IsaLean™ Shake isn't just for drinking anymore. It also makes a great recipe ingredient for foods you can chew!

SHAKE IT GOOD

Add two scoops of IsaLean™ Shake powder to 8 fl. ounces cold purified water in your IsaBlender® or IsaShaker™. Blend or shake well for 30–60 seconds.

NOTE: Follow these same recipes with dairy-free IsaLean™ Shake and IsaLean™ PRO Shake.

Prefer it chilled? Combine ice and cold, purified water to equal 8 fl. ounces.

Like it extra creamy? Blend for 30 seconds, shake contents by hand, then return to blender for another 30 seconds.

Enjoy within 10 minutes of preparing.

LOAD YOUR CUP FROM THE BOTTOM UP!

4 FROZEN INGREDIENTS (includes ice)
Finally, add these for maximum thickness and smoothness.

3 FRESH FRUITS & VEGETABLES (optional)
If desired, add in small cut-up pieces of fruits and veggies.

2 DRY POWDERS AND STICKY INGREDIENTS
Next, add IsaLean™ Shake products, nut butters, extracts, spices, and seeds.

1 WATER OR MILKS
Start with liquid to allow your IsaLean™ Shake to dissolve completely.

CREATE YOUR OWN

Want more variety in your daily shakes? Add extra flavors and textures, while keeping the calories in control.

50 CALORIES OR LESS

Use this as your guide for extra flavor boosters to keep your calories in check if you have specific weight goals.

Calorie-Free Splashes and Dashes

Add a splash or dash of your favorite extract and spice for extra flavor, without the extra calories.

SPLASHES

- Black Coffee
- Extracts (¼ teaspoon)
  - Vanilla
  - Almond
  - Hazelnut
  - Coconut
  - Mint
  - Pumpkin Pie

DASHES

- Cinnamon
- Nutmeg
- Ground Ginger
- Unsweetened Cocoa Powder
- Cayenne Pepper
- Chili Powder

Shake Add-Ins

Choose just 1–2 of the ingredients below to ensure your additions stay under 50 calories.

ADDITIONS:

- Unsweetened Nut Milks: ½ cup
- Low Fat Milk: ¼ cup
- Nut Butters: 1 teaspoon
- Peanut Butter Powder: 1 tablespoon
- Berries: ¼ cup
- Banana: ¼ banana
- Frozen Fruits: ¼ cup
- Avocado: ⅛ cup
- AMPED™ Hydrate: 1 scoop

TIP: Freeze your bananas! Peel them, cut into quarters, and place them in a container in the freezer for convenience.

5 HEALTH BOOSTERS

Maximize your shake's health benefits by adding a scoop of any of these incredible add-ins. Feel free to mix and match based on your personal needs.

IONIX® SUPREME: Helps neutralize stress and body balance†.

ISAGENIX GREENS™: Contains nutrition from over 30 vegetables, herbs, and botanicals for a well-rounded diet.

ISAGENIX FRUITS: Contains antioxidants and phytonutrients from over 30 premium fruits.

IMMUNE SHAKE BOOSTER: Uses immune-health supporting compounds to help strengthen and balance your immune system†.

HEART SHAKE BOOSTER: Contains plant sterol esters to support heart health†.

TIP:
Substitute 100% pure
pumpkin puree in place of
the applesauce to make a
Pumpkin Pie Shake.

Prep time: 3 minutes | **Serves:** 1

Apple Pie Shake

INGREDIENTS

¹/₂ cup unsweetened almond milk

¹/₂ cup cold purified water

2 scoops Creamy French Vanilla IsaLean™ Shake

5 tablespoons unsweetened applesauce

¹/₄ teaspoon vanilla extract

¹/₈ teaspoon ground cinnamon

4 ice cubes

DIRECTIONS

1. In a single-serve blender, add all ingredients in the order listed and blend on high speed for 20 seconds.

NUTRITIONALS PER SERVING: 287 Calories; 6g Fat; 33g Carbs; 10g Fiber; 16g Sugar; 25g Protein

"Has all the flavors of an apple pie. Love the pumpkin idea too!"

Prep time: 3 minutes | **Serves:** 1

Peanut Butter Cup

INGREDIENTS

1 cup cold purified water

2 scoops Creamy Dutch Chocolate IsaLean™ Shake

1 tablespoon peanut butter powder

¹/₄ teaspoon vanilla extract

4 ice cubes

DIRECTIONS

1. In a single-serve blender, add all ingredients in the order listed and blend on high speed for 20 seconds.

NUTRITIONALS PER SERVING: 262 Calories; 7g Fat; 27g Carbs; 9g Fiber; 12g Sugar; 27g Protein

TIP: For even more chocolate flavor, add 1 teaspoon of unsweetened cocoa powder to the shake.

TIP:
For an added
flavor kick, add
¼ teaspoon of
ground cinnamon.

Prep time: 3 minutes | **Serves:** 1

Mocha Shake

INGREDIENTS

½ cup unsweetened almond milk

½ cup strongly-brewed coffee

2 scoops Creamy Dutch Chocolate IsaLean™ Shake

¼ banana

4–6 ice cubes

DIRECTIONS

1. In a single-serve blender, add all ingredients in the order listed and blend on high speed for 20 seconds.

NUTRITIONALS PER SERVING: 284 Calories; 7g Fat; 32g Carbs; 9g Fiber; 16g Sugar; 25g Protein

---

Prep time: 3 minutes | **Serves:** 1

Choco-Mint Berry Shake

INGREDIENTS

1 cup cold purified water

2 scoops Chocolate Mint IsaLean™ Shake

¼ cup frozen blueberries

1 teaspoon unsweetened cocoa powder

DIRECTIONS

1. In a single-serve blender, add all ingredients in the order listed and blend on high speed for 20 seconds.

NUTRITIONALS PER SERVING: 267 Calories; 7g Fat; 29g Carbs; 10g Fiber; 13g Sugar; 25g Protein

TIP: Strawberries or raspberries can be substituted for the blueberries.

TIP:
Frozen peaches can be substituted for the pineapple.

Tropical Shake

INGREDIENTS

¹/₂ cup unsweetened almond milk

¹/₂ cup cold purified water

2 scoops Strawberry Cream IsaLean™ Shake

¹/₄ cup frozen pineapple chunks

¹/₄ teaspoon coconut extract

DIRECTIONS

1. In a single-serve blender, add all ingredients in the order listed and blend on high speed for 20 seconds.

NUTRITIONALS PER SERVING:
288 Calories; 6g Fat; 31g Carbs;
9g Fiber; 16g Sugar; 25g Protein

Strawberry Shortcake Fluff

INGREDIENTS

2 scoops Creamy French Vanilla IsaLean™ Shake

³/₄ cup frozen strawberries

¹/₄ cup unsweetened almond milk

¹/₄ teaspoon vanilla extract

DIRECTIONS

1. Add all ingredients to a food processor in the order listed. Process on high speed for 1¹/₂ minutes, until mixture reaches a fluffy consistency.

NUTRITIONALS PER SERVING:
286 Calories; 6g Fat; 34g Carbs;
11g Fiber; 16g Sugar; 25g Protein

TIP:
This recipe can be split into 2 servings for a perfect snack or dessert.

SHAKES

TIP:
You can make smoothie bowls with any IsaLean™ Shake prepared with ½ cup cold purified water and ¼ cup ice.

Super Smoothie Bowl

INGREDIENTS

2 scoops Vanilla Chai IsaLean™ Shake Dairy-Free

$\frac{1}{2}$ cup cold purified water

$\frac{1}{4}$ cup ice

$\frac{1}{4}$ cup fresh raspberries

$\frac{1}{4}$ cup chopped apple

1 teaspoon sliced almonds, toasted

$\frac{1}{8}$ teaspoon ground cinnamon

DIRECTIONS

1. In a single-serve blender, add IsaLean™ Shake, water, and ice. Blend on high speed for 20 seconds.

2. Pour blended mixture into a serving bowl and top with raspberries, apple, almonds, and cinnamon.

For Chocolate Smoothie Bowl: Any chocolate IsaLean™ Shake, topped with 2 sliced strawberries, 1 teaspoon sliced almonds, and 1 tablespoon toasted unsweetened coconut.

For Strawberry Smoothie Bowl: Any strawberry IsaLean™ Shake, topped with 1 teaspoon cacao nibs, 7 blueberries, and 1 teaspoon rolled oats.

NUTRITIONALS PER SERVING:
297 Calories; 9g Fat; 31g Carbs; 11g Fiber; 12g Sugar; 25g Protein

"I love eating my smoothie with a spoon, especially adding crunchy and fresh fruit toppings!"

TIP:
For blueberry pancakes, fold 1/4 cup fresh blueberries into the batter In step 2.

Prep time: 5 minutes | **Cook time:** 5 minutes | **Serves:** 1

IsaPancakes

INGREDIENTS

2 scoops Creamy French Vanilla IsaLean™ Shake

1 tablespoon gluten-free flour

$\frac{1}{8}$ teaspoon baking powder

$\frac{1}{8}$ teaspoon ground cinnamon

$\frac{1}{4}$ cup unsweetened almond milk

1 large egg white

Coconut oil spray

DIRECTIONS

1. In a bowl, combine IsaLean™ Shake, gluten-free flour, baking powder, and cinnamon. In a separate bowl, whisk together almond milk and egg white until combined.

2. Add the wet ingredients to the dry ingredients, whisking until blended.

3. Heat a nonstick sauté pan over medium heat, then lightly coat with coconut oil spray. To create each pancake, spoon 3 tablespoons of the batter into the hot pan, until all batter has been used. Let cook 2 minutes, flip, and cook on the opposite side for an additional $1\frac{1}{2}$ minutes.

NUTRITIONALS PER SERVING:
291 Calories; 6g Fat; 30g Carbs; 9g Fiber; 11g Sugar; 29g Protein

"I make an extra batch or two and keep them in the freezer for during the week. I just toast a pancake as I need it. Great as a snack or breakfast for the kids!"

Choco-Lava Mug Cake

INGREDIENTS

2 scoops creamy Dutch chocolate IsaLean™ Shake

⅛ teaspoon baking powder

3 tablespoons unsweetened applesauce

3 tablespoons unsweetened almond milk

¼ teaspoon vanilla extract

¼ cup sliced fresh strawberries

DIRECTIONS

1. In a 12-ounce microwave-safe mug, whisk together IsaLean™ Shake and baking powder with a fork. Add applesauce, almond milk, and vanilla extract, whisking until smooth.

2. Microwave on high for 2 minutes. Let cake rest for 1 minute. Garnish with strawberries.

NUTRITIONALS PER SERVING: 276 Calories; 6g Fat; 32g Carbs; 9g Fiber; 16g Sugar; 24g Protein

TIP:
For an even greater treat, place ½ of an IsaDelight® chocolate on top of the cake after cooking.

"This tastes like a lava cake dessert that I would eat at a fine restaurant!"

SNACKS

POWER SNACKS

Crunch, munch, mix, match, and power through your day with help from these well-balanced and calorie-portioned recipes. Or use our handy tips for mixing and matching your proteins with fruits and veggies. They're sure to keep you satisfied between meals and boost your energy.

SMART SNACKING

On a Shake Day, we recommend two snacks per day, each having 100–150 calories. When you are snacking smartly, it will help keep your metabolism going and your blood sugars even.

NOT ALL CALORIES ARE CREATED EQUAL

The ideal snack pack is a combination of the right balance of protein, fat, carbohydrates, and fiber, which will fill you up and boost your energy. The 100- to 150-calorie level is just enough keep you satisfied without going over your daily needs.

Our Isagenix snack options are so convenient, and we've ensured they are delicious and satisfying.

Isagenix Snacks

- ½ IsaLean™ Bar
- ½ IsaLean™ Shake
- 1 package Whey Thins™ or Harvest Thins™
- Fiber Snacks™
- 1–2 IsaDelight®
- 1 Slim Cakes®
- 2 Isagenix Snacks™

ON THE GO?

Keep a stash of Isagenix snacks in your car or office, so instant nutrition is always at your fingertips. You can even toss in some food additions, too!

MAKE YOUR OWN MOVIE SNACK!

- Add $\frac{1}{2}$ IsaLean™ Bar to 1 cup air-popped popcorn

CREATE A "FRESH" TRAIL MIX!

- Add 10 almonds to $\frac{1}{3}$ cup fresh blueberries and 1 IsaDelight®

MIX & MATCH

For your Shake Days, a great snack choice is to start with a protein source and balance with your favorite fruit or vegetable. Here's a list of foods with 100 and 50 calorie counts to keep snack time interesting and fun.

① Start with a PROTEIN

100 CALORIE PROTEIN SOURCES
- 1 tablespoon nut butter
- 1 ounce cheddar cheese
- 1–2 large eggs (75–150 calories)
- 12 large cooked shrimp
- 3 ounces lean, nitrate-free all natural turkey or chicken
- $1/2$ cup plain Greek yogurt
- $1/2$ cup canned salmon
- 12 almonds
- 30 pistachios

② Add a FRUIT OR VEGGIE

100 CALORIE FRUITS
- 1 medium apple
- 1 medium pear
- 1 medium banana
- 28 seedless grapes
- 1 medium orange
- $1/3$ avocado
- 2 cups sliced strawberries
- $1 1/2$ cups blueberries
- 2 mandarin oranges
- $1 1/2$ cups cantaloupe

50 CALORIE VEGGIES
- 12 baby carrots
- $1 1/2$ cups snap peas
- 10 grape tomatoes
- 1 small sweet potato
- 5 mini peppers
- $1 1/2$ cups broccoli
- 3 cups chopped kale
- $1 1/2$ cups Brussels sprouts
- $1 1/2$ cups green beans
- Unlimited celery

TIP: For a 150 calorie snack, have $1/2$ a fruit portion with your protein!

HOUSE FAVORITES

There are a variety of combinations you can choose from! Here are some of our Isagenix Associates' top picks, which also include a combination of Isagenix snacks with your favorite foods. What's so easy is that all of these snacks require minimum or no prep, and the ingredients are easily found in your grocery store.

- $\frac{1}{2}$ apple **+** 1 tablespoon almond or peanut butter

- 1$\frac{1}{2}$ cups snap peas **+** 1 hard-boiled egg

- 5 mini peppers **+** 4 tablespoons hummus

- 10 almonds **+** 1 IsaDelight® **+** $\frac{1}{3}$ cup blueberries

- 3 ounces nitrate-free all natural turkey **+** $\frac{1}{3}$ avocado

- 2 mandarin oranges **+** 30 pistachios

- $\frac{1}{2}$ IsaLean™ Bar **+** 1 cup air-popped popcorn

- 1 package Whey Thins™ **+** $\frac{1}{2}$ pear

TIP:
These can be refrigerated for up to three days, allowing you to prepare your breakfasts in advance.

Prep time: 10 minutes | **Cook time:** 20 minutes | **Makes:** 4 | **Serves:** 2

Egg White Veggie Muffins

INGREDIENTS

6 large egg whites

¼ teaspoon black pepper

⅓ cup thinly sliced button mushrooms

⅓ cup chopped broccoli

¼ cup diced red bell pepper

2 tablespoons shredded cheddar cheese

4 halves sun-dried tomatoes

Olive oil spray

DIRECTIONS

1. Preheat oven to 350°F. Coat 4 cups of a muffin pan with olive oil spray.

2. In a bowl, whisk to combine egg whites and black pepper.

3. Divide mushrooms, broccoli, and bell pepper evenly between the 4 prepared muffin cups. Pour egg white mixture over vegetables, then top each with an equal amount of cheese and 1 sun-dried tomato half.

4. Bake for 20 minutes, or until eggs are set. Serve warm.

NUTRITIONALS PER SERVING:
118 Calories; 3g Fat; 7g Carbs; 2g Fiber; 3g Sugar; 16g Protein

TIP:
This recipe can also be enjoyed as a full meal for one when served with ½ cup of cooked quinoa.

Prep time: 10 minutes | **Serves:** 2

Salmon Lettuce Wraps

INGREDIENTS

½ cup canned wild pink salmon, drained

¼ cup chopped celery

4 halves sun-dried tomatoes, chopped

1 tablespoon extra-virgin olive oil

1 tablespoon chopped fresh basil

2 teaspoons fresh lemon juice

¼ teaspoon garlic powder

2 large lettuce leaves

DIRECTIONS

1. In a mixing bowl, use a fork to gently fold together salmon, celery, sundried tomatoes, olive oil, basil, lemon juice, and garlic powder.

2. Divide mixture evenly between the 2 large leaves of lettuce.

NUTRITIONALS PER SERVING: 160 Calories; 8g Fat; 6g Carbs; 1g Fiber; 3g Sugar; 14g Protein

---

Prep time: 10 minutes | **Cook time:** 10 minutes | **Serves:** 2

Nacho Average Deviled Eggs

INGREDIENTS

2 large hard-boiled eggs, peeled

2 tablespoons nonfat plain Greek yogurt

½ teaspoon fresh lime juice

¼ teaspoon ground cumin

¼ teaspoon chili powder

1 tablespoon reduced-fat shredded cheddar cheese

2 teaspoons chopped fresh cilantro

⅛ teaspoon cayenne pepper

DIRECTIONS

1. Cut peeled eggs in half lengthwise and transfer yolks to a small mixing bowl. Set aside whites.

2. Add yogurt, lime juice, cumin, and chili powder to the yolks and mash with a fork, until combined.

3. Spoon the yolk mixture back into the egg white halves. Top each deviled egg with a sprinkling of cheddar cheese, cilantro, and cayenne pepper.

NUTRITIONALS PER SERVING: 94 Calories; 6g Fat; 1g Carbs; 0g Fiber; 1g Sugar; 9g Protein

TIP:
Want an Italian twist?
Top with sun-dried tomatoes,
goat cheese, and Italian
seasoning

Prep time: 10 minutes | Cook time: 1 minute | Serves: 1

Greek Avocado Toast

INGREDIENTS

1 slice light whole-grain bread

¼ ripe avocado, pitted and peeled

1 teaspoon Isagenix Greens™

¾ teaspoon fresh lemon juice

⅛ teaspoon crushed red pepper flakes

1 grape tomato, quartered

1 tablespoon chopped English cucumber

1 teaspoon crumbled fat-free feta cheese

½ teaspoon chopped fresh dill

DIRECTIONS

1. Toast bread until browned and crisp.

2. In a bowl, combine avocado, Isagenix Greens™, lemon juice, and red pepper flakes, then mash with a fork until chunky but combined.

3. Spread avocado mixture evenly on toast and top with the tomato, cucumber, feta cheese, and dill.

NUTRITIONALS PER SERVING:
148 Calories; 7g Fat; 18g Carbs; 9g Fiber; 2g Sugar, 5g Protein

Prep time: 10 minutes | Makes: 20-24 | Serves: 10-12

Cocoa Protein Balls

INGREDIENTS

2 scoops Creamy Dutch Chocolate IsaLean™ Shake

2 IsaDelight® chocolates, chopped finely

1 cup rolled oats

½ cup natural peanut butter

¼ cup honey

⅓ cup puffed brown rice cereal

¼ teaspoon ground cinnamon

¼ teaspoon unsweetened cocoa powder

2–3 tablespoons hot water

DIRECTIONS

1. Line a sheet pan with wax paper. In a mixing bowl or food processor, fold all ingredients until well combined.

2. Scoop rounded spoonfuls of the mixture and roll into balls, placing on the prepared sheet pan as you go.

3. Cover and refrigerate 1–2 hours before serving.

NUTRITIONALS PER SERVING:
144 Calories; 7g Fat; 15g Carbs; 2g Fiber; 8g Sugar; 6g Protein

TIP:
Pepitas are shelled pumpkin seeds, usually sold near dried fruits in the produce section.

Prep time: 10 minutes | **Cook time:** 55 minutes | **Makes:** 5 (½-cup) servings

IsaHarvest Snack Mix

INGREDIENTS

2 cups frozen peas, thawed

2 teaspoons reduced-sodium tamari soy sauce

1 teaspoon olive oil

¾ teaspoon ground ginger

¾ teaspoon garlic powder

¾ cup puffed brown rice cereal

¼ cup roasted pepitas

¼ cup dried cranberries

1 (0.9 ounce) package Harvest Thins™ Thai Chili

DIRECTIONS

1. Preheat oven to 375°F. Line a baking sheet with aluminum foil.

2. Place thawed peas on paper towels and pat dry. In a mixing bowl, combine peas, tamari sauce, olive oil, ginger, and garlic powder, tossing to evenly coat the peas.

3. Arrange peas in a single layer on the prepared baking sheet and bake 40 minutes, stirring halfway through. Turn oven off and let peas sit in oven for 15 minutes before removing.

4. Cool peas completely, then toss with puffed brown rice, pepitas, dried cranberries, and Harvest Thins™.

5. Store at room temperature in an airtight container.

NUTRITIONALS PER SERVING:
148 Calories; 4g Fat; 20g Carbs; 4g Fiber; 8g Sugar; 8g Protein

"I love the combination of sweet, savory, and spice! Love changing up the recipe with different Whey Thins™, seeds, and dried fruits."

TIP:
For the best presentation,
add a few extra blueberries
to the top of each muffin (along
with the oats) before baking.

Prep time: 10 minutes | **Cook time:** 25 minutes | **Makes:** 6 | **Serves:** 6

Blueberry Oat Muffins

INGREDIENTS

Coconut oil spray

¾ **cup gluten-free flour**

2 scoops Creamy French Vanilla
IsaLean™ Shake

1 teaspoon baking powder

½ cup unsweetened almond milk

¼ cup unsweetened applesauce

2 tablespoons honey

2 tablespoons coconut oil, melted

1 large egg

1 tablespoon lemon zest

1 teaspoon vanilla extract

½ cup fresh blueberries

1 tablespoon rolled oats

DIRECTIONS

1. Preheat oven to 350°F. Lightly coat a 6-cup muffin pan with coconut oil spray.

2. In a mixing bowl, combine flour, IsaLean™ Shake, and baking powder. In a separate bowl, whisk together almond milk, apple sauce, honey, coconut oil, egg, lemon zest, and vanilla extract.

3. Add wet ingredients into the dry ingredients, mixing just until all is combined. Fold in blueberries, but do not overmix.

4. Divide batter evenly between the 6 muffin cups, filling each about ¾ full. Top with the rolled oats.

5. Bake for 25 minutes. Let cool before serving.

NUTRITIONALS PER SERVING:
179 Calories; 7g Fat; 24g Carbs; 4g Fiber; 10g Sugar; 7g Protein

TIP:
For more flavor, sprinkle ¼ teaspoon of ground cinnamon and ¼ teaspoon of unsweetened cocoa powder over the second layer of yogurt before topping with the other ingredients. Shown: ½ Chocolate Decadence IsaLean™ Bar.

Prep time: 5 minutes | **Serves:** 1

IsaLean™ Bar Parfait

INGREDIENTS

⅓ **cup nonfat plain Greek yogurt**

½ **(any flavor) IsaLean™ Bar, chopped**

¼ **cup fresh raspberries**

DIRECTIONS

1. Spoon half of the yogurt into a small parfait dish.

2. Top yogurt with ½ of the chopped IsaLean™ Bar and ½ of the raspberries.

3. Spoon a second layer of yogurt into the parfait dish and top with the remaining chopped IsaLean™ Bar and strawberries.

NUTRITIONALS PER SERVING:
180 Calories; 3g Fat; 22g Carbs; 2g Fiber; 13g Sugar; 17g Protein

All of our carefully
crafted meal recipes
contain balanced nutrition,
400- to 600-calories per
serving, and incredible flavor.
If that wasn't enough, they're
also quick to make and simple
to clean up.

MEALS

4 EASY STEPS TO A BALANCED MEAL

Use this easy guide to help you create your own balanced
400- to 600-calorie meal.

1 Pick a variety of **VEGETABLES**

Portion Size: 2+ cups or size of 2 fists

- Roasted Veggies
- Tossed Salad
- Steamed Veggies
- Soup

PORTION SIZE:
2 Fists

2 Add a **LEAN PROTEIN**

Portion Size: 4–6 oz. or ½ cup or size of palm of hand

- Beans/Legumes
- Organic Poultry
- Grass-Fed Beef
- Omega-3 Eggs
- Low-Mercury Seafood

PORTION SIZE:
Palm of Hand

3 Add **WHOLE-GRAINS**

Portion Size: ½ cup cooked or size of fist

- Brown Rice
- Quinoa
- Farro
- Whole-Wheat Pasta
- High Fiber Tortilla
- Sweet Potato

PORTION SIZE:
1 Fist

4 Include a **HEALTHY FAT**

Portion Size: 1 serving or size of thumb

- 2 teaspoons Oil (olive or canola)
- 1 tablespoon Seeds
- 1 tablespoon Nuts
- ¼ Avocado

PORTION SIZE:
Thumb

TIP:
Shrimp or chicken can be substituted for the sirloin.

Prep time: 10 minutes | **Cook time:** 10 minutes | **Serves:** 2

Asian Beef Stir Fry With Rice Noodles

INGREDIENTS

2 ounces dried rice noodles

1 tablespoon olive oil

12 ounces sirloin steak, cut into thin 2-inch strips

¹/₂ cup snow peas, trimmed

¹/₂ cup carrots, cut into ¹/₄-inch sticks

³/₄ cup water

2 tablespoons all-fruit orange marmalade

2 tablespoons reduced-sodium tamari soy sauce

1¹/₂ teaspoons minced fresh ginger

³/₄ teaspoon sesame seeds

¹/₄ teaspoon crushed red pepper flakes

DIRECTIONS

1. Cook rice noodles according to package instructions. Set aside.

2. Heat olive oil in a skillet over medium-high heat. Add sirloin steak and let cook 2 minutes, flipping once.

3. Add snow peas and carrots to the steak and stir fry for 4 minutes.

4. Add rice noodles, water, orange marmalade, tamari sauce, ginger, sesame seeds, and crushed red pepper flakes to the stir fry and let cook an additional 4 minutes, stirring constantly, just until snow peas are tender.

NUTRITIONALS PER SERVING:
600 Calories; 29g Fat; 43g Carbs; 4g Fiber; 11g Sugar; 40g Protein

"Everyone enjoyed this recipe, even the kids! I simply doubled everything to cook for the whole family."

TIP:
For a spicy kick, add
¼ teaspoon cayenne
pepper to the seasoning
on the chicken.

Prep time: 10 minutes | **Cook time:** 20 minutes | **Serves:** 2

One-Pan Chicken Fajitas

INGREDIENTS

Olive oil spray

2 (6-ounce) boneless, skinless chicken breasts, cut into ¼-inch strips

1 tablespoon lime juice

1 teaspoon olive oil

1 teaspoon ground cumin

1 teaspoon chili powder

½ teaspoon garlic powder

¼ teaspoon each salt and black pepper

1 red bell pepper, seeded and cut into ¼-inch strips

1 small zucchini, cut into ¼-inch strips

½ medium yellow onion, cut into ¼-inch strips

6 (5-inch) soft corn tortillas, warmed

½ cup fresh salsa

½ cup shredded reduced-fat cheddar cheese

DIRECTIONS

1. Preheat oven to 375°F. Line a sheet pan with aluminum foil, then lightly spray with olive oil spray.

2. In a mixing bowl, toss chicken in lime juice, olive oil, cumin, chili powder, garlic powder, salt, and black pepper. Place seasoned chicken onto the prepared sheet pan in a single layer.

3. Arrange bell pepper, zucchini, and onion on baking sheet beside the chicken. Lightly spray vegetables with olive oil spray.

4. Bake for 20 minutes, or until chicken is cooked through and vegetables are tender.

5. When serving, split chicken and vegetables evenly over each tortilla and top with salsa and cheese.

NUTRITIONALS PER SERVING:
496 Calories; 12g Fat; 43g Carbs; 5g Fiber; 5g Sugar; 51g Protein

"A huge hit in my house, plus easy cleanup. Doubled the recipe for my family."

TIP:
Use a single-serve blender or food processor to crush the Whey Thins™ for finer crumbs.

Prep time: 10 minutes | **Cook time:** 25 minutes | **Serves:** 2

Whey Better Chicken Dinner

INGREDIENTS

2 (0.9 ounce) package cheddar Whey Thins™, finely crushed

1 large egg

2 tablespoons water

6 (2-ounce) chicken tenderloins

1¹/₂ teaspoons paprika

1 cup broccoli florets

1 cup baby potatoes, halved

1 cup fresh green beans, trimmed and halved

1 tablespoon olive oil

1 teaspoon dried thyme

2 teaspoons minced garlic

¹/₄ teaspoon each salt and black pepper

DIRECTIONS

1. Preheat oven to 375°F. Line a sheet pan with aluminum foil.

2. Place finely crushed Whey Thins™ in a wide bowl. In a separate wide bowl, whisk together egg and water to create an egg wash.

3. Place each chicken tenderloin into the egg wash, then into the crumbs to coat, shaking off any excess. Place breaded chicken onto the prepared sheet pan in a single layer. Sprinkle with paprika.

4. In a mixing bowl, toss together broccoli, potatoes, green beans, olive oil, thyme, garlic, salt, and pepper.

5. Arrange vegetable mixture on the prepared sheet pan beside the breaded chicken.

6. Bake for 25 minutes, or until potatoes are tender and chicken is cooked through.

NUTRITIONALS PER SERVING:
428 Calories, 13g Fat; 29g Carbs; 4g Fiber; 2g Sugar; 48g Protein

Prep time: 15 minutes | **Serves:** 2

IsaSalad

INGREDIENTS
Dressing

1 scoop Isagenix Greens™

1 scoop Creamy French Vanilla IsaLean™ Shake

³/₄ cup grapefruit, peeled and seeded

¹/₄ cup olive oil

2¹/₂ tablespoons water

1¹/₂ tablespoons red wine vinegar

¹/₈ teaspoon black pepper

Salad

4 cups salad greens

4 ounces nitrate-free oven-roasted turkey breast, chopped

2 hard-boiled eggs, peeled and quartered

12 cherry tomatoes, halved

¹/₂ avocado, peeled and chopped

2 (0.9 ounce) packages Barbecue Whey Thins™

DIRECTIONS

1. To create the IsaDressing: Add Greens™, IsaLean™ Shake, grapefruit, olive oil, water, vinegar, and pepper to a single-serve blender and blend on high speed for 10 seconds. Set aside.

2. Divide salad greens, turkey, egg, tomatoes, avocado, and Whey Thins™ evenly between two serving bowls. Top each salad with 3 tablespoons of the salad dressing before serving.

NUTRITIONALS PER SERVING:
440 Calories; 24g Fat; 26g Carbs; 7g Fiber; 9g Sugar; 34g Protein

TIP:
Make your tomato sauce ahead of time and use it for a variety of meals throughout the week.

Prep time: 15 minutes | **Cook time:** 25 minutes | **Serves:** 2

Light Chicken Parm Dinner

INGREDIENTS

¹/₄ cup Classic Tomato Sauce recipe (see page: 78)

2 (6-ounce) boneless, skinless chicken breasts

1 tablespoon plus 1 teaspoon olive oil, divided

2 tablespoons grated Parmesan cheese

¹/₂ teaspoon Italian seasoning

3 cups eggplant, cut into ¹/₄-inch thick "fries"

¹/₂ teaspoon dried oregano

¹/₄ teaspoon each salt and black pepper

3 cups broccoli florets, cut into ¹/₂-inch thick pieces

Olive oil spray

¹/₄ cup shredded part-skim mozzarella cheese

DIRECTIONS

1. Prepare Classic Tomato Sauce according to recipe directions.

2. Preheat oven to 375°F. Line a sheet pan with aluminum foil.

3. Place chicken on prepared sheet pan and brush each piece with ¹/₂ teaspoon olive oil before topping with equal amount of the Parmesan cheese and Italian seasoning.

4. In a mixing bowl, toss together eggplant, 1 tablespoon olive oil, oregano, salt, and pepper, until evenly coated.

5. Arrange broccoli and coated eggplant fries in a single layer on the baking sheet beside the chicken. Lightly mist broccoli with olive oil spray. Bake for 20 minutes.

6. Top each chicken breast with 2 tablespoons tomato sauce and 2 tablespoons mozzarella cheese. Bake an additional 5 minutes, or until cheese is melted and chicken is cooked throughout.

NUTRITIONALS PER SERVING:
420 Calories; 16g Fat; 17g Carbs; 9g Fiber; 5g Sugar; 52g Protein

TIP:
Sweet potatoes can be used in place of the butternut squash, if desired.

Prep time: 10 minutes | **Cook time:** 12 minutes | **Serves:** 2

Hearty Chicken and Butternut Squash

INGREDIENTS

1 tablespoon olive oil

2 cups peeled and ($\frac{1}{4}$-inch) cubed butternut squash

2 (6-ounce) boneless, skinless chicken breasts

$\frac{2}{3}$ cup low-sodium chicken broth

$\frac{1}{2}$ cup fresh green beans, trimmed

$\frac{1}{2}$ cup walnut halves

8 cherry tomatoes

1 teaspoon dried thyme

1 teaspoon minced garlic

$\frac{1}{4}$ teaspoon each salt and black pepper

DIRECTIONS

1. Heat olive oil in a skillet over medium-high heat. Add butternut squash and sauté for 5 minutes, stirring occasionally.

2. Add chicken to the skillet and cook for $1\frac{1}{2}$ minutes per side, or until golden brown.

3. Add chicken broth, green beans, walnuts, cherry tomatoes, thyme, garlic, salt, and pepper to the skillet and toss to combine. Cover skillet, and let cook for 4 minutes, or until green beans are tender and chicken is cooked throughout.

NUTRITIONALS PER SERVING:
520 Calories; 28g Fat; 28g Carbs; 6g Fiber; 7g Sugar; 48g Protein

TIP:
Want an added flavor kick?
Spread 1 teaspoon honey
mustard over each piece
of salmon before baking.

Prep time: 10 minutes | **Cook time:** 20 minutes | **Serves:** 2

Spicy Salmon With Zucchini

INGREDIENTS

Olive oil spray

2 (5-ounce) fresh wild salmon fillets, about 1¼-inches thick, skin off

¼ teaspoon each salt and black pepper, divided

4 (¼-inch thick) lemon slices

2 cups zucchini, cut in half lengthwise and into ½-inch pieces

¼ small red onion, thinly sliced

⅔ cup cherry tomatoes

1 small jalapeño pepper, seeded and thinly sliced

1 tablespoon olive oil

½ teaspoon ground coriander

¼ teaspoon dried oregano

1 cup cooked whole-grain brown rice

DIRECTIONS

1. Preheat oven to 400°F. Line a sheet pan with aluminum foil and lightly spray with olive oil spray.

2. Place salmon on the prepared sheet pan and lightly season with pinches of the salt and pepper. Place 2 lemon slices over top each seasoned fillet.

3. In a mixing bowl, toss together zucchini, red onion, cherry tomatoes, jalapeño, olive oil, coriander, oregano, and the remaining salt and pepper.

4. Arrange zucchini mixture on the sheet pan beside the salmon.

5. Bake for 20 minutes, or until salmon is cooked through and flakes easily with a fork. Serve alongside cooked brown rice.

NUTRITIONALS PER SERVING:
408 Calories; 17g Fat; 31g Carbs; 4g Fiber; 5g Sugar; 33g Protein

TIP:
10 ounces of boneless, skinless chicken thighs or chicken breasts can be substituted for the pork.

Prep time: 10 minutes | **Cook time:** 30 minutes | **Serves:** 2

Savory Mustard Pork Tenderloin

INGREDIENTS

1 tablespoon olive oil

10 ounces pork tenderloin, cut into $1/2$-inch pieces

3 cups finely chopped Swiss chard, stems removed

2 cups low-sodium chicken broth

$1/2$ cup white quinoa

$1/2$ cup chopped yellow onion

2 tablespoons whole-grain mustard

2 tablespoons apple cider vinegar

1 tablespoon tomato paste

2 teaspoons light brown sugar

2 teaspoons Worcestershire sauce

DIRECTIONS

1. Heat olive oil in a sauce pot over medium-high heat. Add pork and brown on all sides, about 5 minutes.

2. Add Swiss chard, chicken broth, quinoa, onion, mustard, vinegar, tomato paste, brown sugar, and Worcestershire sauce to the pot and bring up to a simmer. Reduce heat to medium-low, cover pot, and let cook for 20 minutes, or until quinoa is tender.

NUTRITIONALS PER SERVING:
484 Calories; 19g Fat; 44g Carbs; 5g Fiber; 12g Sugar; 37 g Protein

TIP:
For an extra zesty
flavor, squeeze the juice
of ½ lemon over top
before serving.

Prep time: 10 minutes | **Cook time:** 8 ½ minutes | **Serves:** 2

Shrimp and Cauliflower Fried Rice

INGREDIENTS

1 tablespoon olive oil

16 large raw shrimp, peeled and deveined

1 ½ tablespoons sesame oil

1 (12-ounce) package frozen riced cauliflower

¾ cup low-sodium vegetable broth

1 cup diced carrot

½ cup frozen peas

2 teaspoons minced fresh ginger

2 teaspoons minced garlic

4 scallions, chopped

1 tablespoon reduced-sodium tamari soy sauce

DIRECTIONS

1. Heat olive oil in a large skillet over medium-high heat. Add shrimp and cook, stirring occasionally, for 1 ½ minutes. Remove from skillet and set aside.

3. Add sesame oil, riced cauliflower, vegetable broth, carrots, peas, ginger, and garlic to the skillet and stir fry for 6 minutes, or until carrots are tender.

4. Return the shrimp to the skillet and add scallions and tamari sauce. Stir fry 1 additional minute before serving.

NUTRITIONALS PER SERVING:
376 Calories; 20g Fat; 25g Carbs; 8g Fiber; 10g Sugar; 27g Protein

"I can cook this in less than 10 minutes. Love to change it up by using boneless chicken breast or thinly sliced steak."

TIP:
Canned garbanzo beans (drained and rinsed) can be substituted for the cannellini beans.

Prep time: 10 minutes | **Cook time:** 25 minutes | **Serves:** 2

Sweet Potato, Kale, and White Bean Stew

INGREDIENTS

1 tablespoon olive oil

2 cups sweet potatoes, peeled and cut into $1/4$-inch pieces

$1/2$ cup celery, cut into $1/4$-inch pieces

$1/2$ cup chopped yellow onion

$2\,1/2$ cups low-sodium vegetable broth

2 cups finely chopped kale, stems removed

1 (15.5-ounce) can cannellini beans, drained and rinsed

2 teaspoons minced fresh sage

2 teaspoons minced garlic

$1/4$ teaspoon black pepper

1 avocado, pitted, peeled, and chopped

DIRECTIONS

1. Heat olive oil in a sauce pot over medium-high heat. Add sweet potatoes, celery, and onion to the pot and sauté for 5 minutes, just until onions are translucent.

2. Reduce heat to medium and stir in vegetable broth, kale, cannellini beans, sage, garlic, and pepper. Let cook, stirring occasionally, for 20 minutes, or until sweet potatoes are tender.

3. Serve topped with chopped avocado.

NUTRITIONALS PER SERVING:
547 Calories; 21g Fat; 84g Carbs; 27g Fiber; 12g Sugar; 18g Protein

TIP:
While any cooked brown rice can be used, for the best texture in this recipe, use "Ready Rice" sold precooked in pouches in the rice aisle.

Prep time: 10 minutes | **Cook time:** 15 minutes | **Serves:** 2

Thai Chicken and Rice Bowl

INGREDIENTS

1 tablespoon olive oil

2 (6-ounce) boneless, skinless chicken breasts, cut into 1-inch pieces

1 cup chopped yellow onion

¾ cup low-sodium chicken broth

⅔ cup frozen peas

¼ cup lite coconut milk

2 tablespoons lime juice

2½ teaspoons curry powder

2 cups frozen chopped spinach

1 cup brown "Ready Rice" (see tip)

¼ cup chopped fresh cilantro

¼ teaspoon black pepper

DIRECTIONS

1. Heat olive oil in a skillet over medium-high heat. Add chicken and onions and sauté for 5 minutes.

2. Add chicken broth, peas, coconut milk, lime juice, and curry powder to the skillet and, stirring occasionally, let cook 5 minutes.

3. Stir in spinach, brown "Ready Rice", cilantro, and pepper. Cover skillet and let cook 5 additional minutes before serving.

NUTRITIONALS PER SERVING:
406 Calories; 12g Fat; 31g Carbs; 5g Fiber; 3g Sugar; 45g Protein

TIP:
Frozen mango can be used in place of fresh—just thaw prior to using. Peaches are also a good alternative.

Prep time: 10 minutes | **Cook time:** 20 minutes | **Serves:** 2

Tropical Cod With Asparagus

INGREDIENTS

Olive oil spray

2 (6-ounce) fresh wild cod fillets, about 1-inch thick, skin off

20 spears fresh asparagus, stalks trimmed

$\frac{1}{8}$ teaspoon each salt and black pepper

$\frac{1}{2}$ cup chopped ripe mango

$\frac{1}{2}$ cup chopped cucumber

8 cherry tomatoes, halved

1 tablespoon extra-virgin olive oil

1 tablespoon lime juice

2 teaspoons minced jalapeño

1 teaspoon minced mint or parsley

1 cup cooked farro

DIRECTIONS

1. Preheat oven to 400°F. Line a sheet pan with aluminum foil and lightly spray with olive oil spray.

2. Place cod and asparagus on the prepared sheet pan, lightly mist with olive oil spray, and season with the salt and pepper.

3. Bake for 20 minutes, or until cod is cooked through and flakes easily with a fork.

4. Meanwhile, in a mixing bowl, toss together mango, cucumber, cherry tomatoes, olive oil, lime juice, jalapeño, and mint to create a mango salsa.

5. Serve the baked cod and asparagus alongside the mango salsa with a side of cooked farro.

NUTRITIONALS PER SERVING:
384 Calories; 9g Fat; 41g Carbs; 8g Fiber; 12g Sugar; 38g Protein

TIP:
If you do not have small baking dishes or ramekins on hand, this recipe can also be made in a 9-inch by 5-inch loaf pan.

Prep time: 15 minutes | **Cook time:** 30 minutes | **Serves:** 4

Turkey Enchilada Bakes

INGREDIENTS

Olive oil spray

1 tablespoon olive oil

1 pound lean ground turkey

$\frac{1}{2}$ cup chopped yellow onion

$\frac{1}{4}$ green bell pepper, chopped

1 (8-ounce) can tomato sauce

$\frac{1}{4}$ cup frozen corn kernels

2 tablespoons chopped
fresh cilantro

1 teaspoon ground cumin

4 (5-inch) soft corn tortillas,
cut into quarters

$\frac{1}{2}$ cup reduced-fat shredded
cheddar cheese

DIRECTIONS

1. Preheat oven to 350°F. Spray 4 (8-ounce) ramekins or small baking dishes with olive oil spray.

2. Heat olive oil in a sauce pot over medium-high heat. Add ground turkey and brown, crumbling as it cooks, for 7 minutes. Add onion and bell pepper to the skillet and sauté for 3 minutes.

3. Stir in tomato sauce, corn, cilantro, and cumin. Bring up to a simmer and remove from heat.

4. Build 4 individual casseroles by layering two cuts of the tortillas on the bottom of each prepared ramekin. Top tortillas with $\frac{1}{3}$ cup of the turkey mixture. Top the turkey mixture with 1 tablespoon cheddar cheese.

5. Repeat the last step to create a second layer in each ramekin as you use the remaining tortillas, turkey mixture, and cheese. Bake for 30 minutes or until bubbly and hot.

NUTRITIONALS PER SERVING:
396 Calories; 24g Fat; 21g Carbs; 3g Fiber; 3g Sugar; 25g Protein

TIP:
For a spicier chili, add ½ teaspoon crushed red pepper flakes in the first step.

Prep time: 10 minutes | **Cook time:** 20 minutes | **Serves:** 4

Vegetarian Chili

INGREDIENTS

1 (15.5-ounce) can red kidney beans, drained and rinsed

1 (14.5-ounce) can fire-roasted diced tomatoes

1 (8-ounce) can tomato sauce

1 cup low-sodium vegetable broth

1 cup chopped carrots

1 cup frozen chopped peppers and onions

1/2 cup frozen corn kernels

2 tablespoons chili powder

1 1/2 teaspoons ground cumin

1 teaspoon light brown sugar

1 teaspoon dried oregano

1/4 teaspoon each salt and black pepper

4 cups cooked brown rice

DIRECTIONS

1. Place all ingredients, except brown rice, into a sauce pot over medium-high heat, stirring to combine.

2. Bring mixture up to a simmer, cover, and reduce heat to medium-low.

3. Let cook for 25 minutes, stirring occasionally. Serve over or alongside cooked brown rice.

NUTRITIONALS PER SERVING:
452 Calories; 2g Fat; 98g Carbs; 17g Fiber; 13g Sugar; 14g Protein

"This was so simple to prepare, but it sure didn't taste simple!"

TIP:
Combine ¼ cup nonfat plain Greek yogurt with 2 tablespoons of pesto sauce for a quick dressing for 2.

Prep time: 15 minutes | **Cook time:** 10 minutes | **Serves:** 2

Veggie Burger Bowl

INGREDIENTS

1 cup reduced-sodium black beans, drained and rinsed

$^3/_4$ cup cooked brown rice

$^1/_2$ cup chopped cooked beets

3 tablespoons rolled oats

3 tablespoons minced onion

1 large egg white

2$^1/_2$ teaspoons smoked paprika

$^1/_4$ teaspoon each salt and black pepper

1 tablespoon olive oil

4 cups salad greens

$^1/_2$ cup cherry tomato halves

$^1/_2$ cup chopped cucumber

$^1/_2$ cup shredded carrots

DIRECTIONS

1. In a mixing bowl, mash black beans. Add rice, beets, oats, onion, egg white, smoked paprika, salt, and pepper to the beans and fold until all is combined. Form into 2 patties.

2. Heat olive oil in a skillet over medium heat. Add patties to the skillet, cover, and let cook for 5 minutes on each side.

3. Divide salad greens between two serving dishes and top with an equal amount of the tomatoes, cucumber, and carrots. Serve veggie burger over salad. Drizzle with a low-calorie dressing or vinegar, if desired.

NUTRITIONALS PER SERVING:
406 Calories; 11g Fat; 68g Carbs; 14g Fiber; 11g Sugar; 16g Protein

TIP:
To make this recipe gluten-free, use gluten-free bread crumbs and serve over zucchini noodles (1 medium zucchini per serving). Zucchini noodles also reduce the recipe by 140 calories.

Prep time: 10 minutes | Cook time: 20 minutes | Serves: 2

Classic Spaghetti and Turkey Meatballs

INGREDIENTS

1 batch Classic Tomato Sauce recipe (see page 78)

12 ounces extra-lean ground turkey

3 tablespoons Italian-seasoned breadcrumbs (see tip)

2 tablespoons grated Parmesan cheese

1 large egg

1/2 teaspoon dried oregano

1/2 teaspoon garlic powder

1/2 teaspoon black pepper

4 ounces whole-wheat spaghetti (see tip)

DIRECTIONS

1. Prepare Classic Tomato Sauce according to the recipe directions.

2. In a mixing bowl, combine ground turkey, breadcrumbs, Parmesan cheese, egg, oregano, garlic, and pepper. Divide the mixture evenly and form into 6 meatballs.

3. Add meatballs to the prepared tomato sauce, cover, and bring up to a simmer. Reduce to medium heat and let cook for 20 minutes, until meatballs are cooked through.

4. Meanwhile, cook spaghetti according to the package directions. Drain well before serving, and top with the meatballs and sauce.

NUTRITIONALS PER SERVING:
600 Calories; 16g Fat; 63g Carbs; 9g Fiber; 10g Sugar; 59g Protein

Classic Tomato Sauce

INGREDIENTS

1 tablespoon extra-virgin olive oil

1 tablespoon minced fresh garlic

1 (15-ounce) can crushed tomatoes

¼ cup chopped fresh basil

**¼ teaspoon each salt and
black pepper**

DIRECTIONS

1. Heat olive oil in a 2-quart sauce pot over medium heat. Add garlic and cook for 2 minutes, stirring frequently.

2. Add crushed tomatoes, basil, salt, and pepper to the pot and bring up to a simmer. Reduce heat to medium-low and let simmer, stirring occasionally, for 20 minutes.

NUTRITIONALS PER SERVING:
66 Calories; 4g Fat; 8g Carbs; 2g Fiber; 4g Sugar; 25g Protein

TIP:
This freezes well and can easily be doubled to prepare plenty of sauce for future meals.

CLEANSES

CLEANSE WITH BENEFITS

In addition to the product directions for deep and everyday cleansing, these recipes will provide you with new ways for you to look forward to your Cleanse Days. Cleanse for Life® is scientifically formulated to support whole-body cleansing and protect against the effects of oxidative stress and harmful toxins†.

TIP:
Split the batch between 4 mason jars or water bottles for the day to make it easy to follow your cleanse schedule.

Cleanse Day Punch

INGREDIENTS

16 ounces Cleanse for Life®

2 ounces Ionix® Supreme

1 Apple Pomegranate e+™ energy shot

1 stick Refreshing Grape AMPED™ Hydrate

Cold purified water

Ice

DIRECTIONS

1. In a tall pitcher, mix all ingredients, except ice, stirring until combined. Add ice and enough purified water to fill the pitcher to 64 ounces.

2. Divide punch into 4 equal servings to be used for your Cleanse Day.

NUTRITIONALS PER SERVING:
76 Calories; 0g Fat; 19g Carbs;
1g Fiber; 15g Sugar; 0g Protein

Grape-Berry Cleanse

INGREDIENTS

4 ounces Cleanse for Life®

1/2 stick Refreshing Grape AMPED™ Hydrate

1/2 cup cold purified water

8 ice cubes

DIRECTIONS

1. In a tall glass, mix all ingredients, except ice, stirring until combined.

2. Stir in ice cubes before serving.

NUTRITIONALS PER SERVING:
75 Calories; 0g Fat; 19g Carbs;
1g Fiber; 16g Sugar; 0g Protein

TIP:
For a change of flavor, try using Lemon Lime AMPED™ Hydrate.

CLEANSES

TIP:
You can simply make the
Sparkler a Cleanse Day drink
by adding 2 more ounces of
Cleanse for Life® to this recipe.

Prep time: 3 minutes | **Serves:** 1

Everyday Cleanse Sparkler

INGREDIENTS

2 ounces Cleanse for Life®

1 scoop Isagenix Fruits

1 cup cold sparkling water

4-6 ice cubes

DIRECTIONS

1. In a tall glass, mix all ingredients, except ice, stirring until combined.

2. Stir in ice cubes before serving.

NUTRITIONALS PER SERVING:
45 Calories; 0g Fat; 10g Carbs;
1g Fiber; 5g Sugar; 0g Protein

"This cleanse drink is so refreshing! Love it!"

Prep time: 3 minutes | **Serves:** 1

Everyday Ginger-Infused Cleanse Tea

INGREDIENTS

½ cup purified water

1 teaspoon thinly sliced ginger

2 ounces Cleanse for Life®

DIRECTIONS

1. Add water and ginger to a microwave-safe mug.

2. Microwave until hot, about 1 minute 15 seconds.

3. Let rest for 2 minutes before stirring in Cleanse for Life®.

NUTRITIONALS PER SERVING:
22 Calories; 0g Fat; 5g Carbs;
0g Fiber; 4g Sugar; 0g Protein

TIP:
Try infusing 1-2 tablespoons of fresh chopped mint leaves in place of the ginger.

Behold, The Bedtime Belly Buster!

This exclusive—and wildly popular—Bedtime Belly Buster (BBB) is an Isagenix Associate-inspired creation, developed as a convenient way to release stubborn belly fat*. Enjoy this high-protein, nutrient-dense treat 30–60 minutes before bedtime.

Prep time: 3 minutes | **Serves:** 1

INGREDIENTS

1 scoop (any flavor) IsaPro®

1 serving Isagenix Fruit or Isagenix Greens™

4–5 ounces cold purified water

Ice (optional)

DIRECTIONS

1. Add all ingredients, except ice, to a single-serve blender or shaker cup.

2. Blend or shake for 30–60 seconds, until fully combined. Drink over ice, if desired.

NUTRITIONALS PER SERVING:
120 Calories; 2g Fat; 7g Carbs; 3g Fiber; 2g Sugar; 19g Protein

TIP:
Don't forget to use Sleep Support and Renewal™ spray immediately before bedtime to assist with a restful night's sleep.